"DR. BOB'S"

CD

CATALOG

(in B&W)

by Robert W. Blake

ISBN-13:978-1516981702
ISBN-10:1516981708

HERE IS A LIST OF MY CDS AND THE SONGS THAT ARE ON EACH, ALONG WITH THE PUBLIC DOMAIN SONGS THAT I HAVE RECORDED ALSO IN THE LIST ARE SOME TEACHING CDS THAT I HAVE DONE.

Robert W. Blake

This QR code will take you my cdbaby.com web page where you will be able to sample or purchase most of the items In this catalog.
For those that are not on the web page just type the title of the item in the search boxes of cdbaby.com, I-Tunes, Amzon or Spotify.
If you do not have a QR Code reader/scanner just type the title of the item in the search boxes of cdbaby.com, I-Tunes, Amazon or Spotify.
The point of the QR code is that it takes you to most of my works at one place so you don't have to type in each item.

This QR code will take you to my
createspace.com web page
where you will find my books.
Each CD title has a corresponding book title
with the lyrics, melody line
and chords. There are also instruction books on
Guitar, Songwriting, How to boost your
songwriting-performing and
recording career, Children's books and a
Two-Volume Set
about the story of my life in music.
(I'm still working on Volume Three)
If you do not have a QR reader/scanner, just type
the item title into one of the following Search
Boxes; createspace.com, amazon.com, kindle,
Barnes & Noble or Walden Books.

Any Place Is Home To Me.

Songs: Any Place Is Home To me, Sing A Little Song, I Am Me, By The Numbers, Jamaican Girl, Love Land, Lullaby Shuffle And Swing, My Hang-Up, Once Upon A Time, Lord I'm Lonesome Tonight, Amanda The Panda, Paula The Koala Bear, Can You Imagine Christmas In Australia. Bonus Songs: Fort Lauderdale & Massachusetts.

GOOD FOOD, GOOD PEOPLE & GOOD TIMES

BOB BLAKE
aka/"Dr. Bob"
(The Music Doctor)

Good Food, Good People & Good Times.

Songs: Good Food, Good People & Good Times,
Flyin' By The Seat Of Her Pants, You Lied, The Lady From
Trinidad, She's A Woman, I Can Hear The Banjo Ringin',
You're No Good For Me, Day After Day.

LUCKY TO BE ME

BOB BLAKE aka/"Dr. Bob"
(The Music Doctor)

Lucky To Be Me.

Songs: Lucky To Be Me, America *(The Land Where Freedom
Always Rings),* Honky Tonk Round, Love's Supposed To Come
Easy, After All Is Said And Done, Hope & Dreams & Love &
Music, Tools Of The Trade, Hey Cat You Stray Cat,
Honky Tonk Tail-Gate Tour, I Just Can't Help Lovin' That Girl Of

"DR. BOB'S"
5 Original
Christmas Songs
See back for song
listing

© 20006 by Robert Blake

"Dr. Bob's" 5 Original Christmas Songs.

SUMMER MAN
BOB BLAKE
aka/"Dr. Bob"
(The Music Doctor)
INSTRUMENTALS

Summer Man.

Songs: Summer Man, Questions, Jiggers, Bob's Minor Cant,Trippin', Bouzouki Song, Flyin' Fingers, Hammerin' Axes,The Haunting, The Song Of The Islands, Ramblin', Incantation,Hammerin' Axes 2, Boppin' The Blues.

A Whole Mess O' Blues.

Songs: A Whole Mess O' Blues, I Can't Forget About You, Sorry That You Are Gone Blues, Boogie Blues Shuffle, High School Ring, No Nonsense Blues, Tom Cat, Bouncing Baby Blues, Sunrise Blues, Swingin' Country Blues, Major Minor Country Blues, Blue Tango, The Optomist, Miami Blues Shuffle, Dr. Bob's Boogie, Low Down Blues.

BLAKEOLOGY

BOB BLAKE

aka/"Dr. Bob"(The Music Doctor)

Blakeology.

Songs: Blakeology, Signed, Sealed & Delivered, Passion de Dance, Wonders, Southern Comfort, Manatee Harbour, Sailing Home, Help Me See The Light, American Indian, "Dr. Bob's"Good-Time Band, I Don't Know, Happy Birthday Song, Ode To Loving You, Back To Our Youth, Life, When I Reach The Promised Land, Life Of Love, Blakeology II.

ROMPIN'
With "DR. BOB"
BOB BLAKE
aka/"Dr. Bob"(The Music Doctor)

© Copyright 2006 by Robert Blake

Rompin' With "Dr. Bob".

Songs: Rompin', Taylor's Tune, Lovin' It, Crammin, Ghosts & Goblins, Bright Sunny Day,
Skippin' Bright Shining Star, Celtic Lady, Country Time, Confusion, Jungle Queen, Perception, Sliding, In Old Sicily, Highlander, Lunar Sea, Cape Breton Isle, The Land Of Ire.

YEAH, MAN!!!

BONUS SONG:
NO U-TURN

BOB BLAKE
aka/"Dr. Bob" (The Music Doctor)

Yeah, Man!!!

Songs: Yeah, Man!!!, The Carpeteria Song, Hold On Tight Babe, Running Fingers, The Great Alaska Earthquake Of 1964, Ups And Downs, Halleluja, Glory, Itty Bitty Pretty Bitty Baby, Real Hot Kitty, Just Another Face In The Crowd. Bonus Song: No U-Turn.

WRITE IT DOWN
(The Battle Cry of
Song Writers the World 'round)

BONUS SONG:
ALL THE WAY RED SOX

BOB BLAKE
aka/"Dr. Bob" *(The Music Doctor)*

Write It Down.

Songs: Write It Down, (The Battle Cry of Songwriters The World 'round), Too Many Crazies On The Road, Meet Me At Kaye Stevens Park, Ode To The North, Let's Make A Toast, Long Legged Cat, I'm In Love, The Cleopatra Blues, I'll Tell You In A Song, The Florida Keys, You've Got To Hear What People Say, The Way That I Feel.

SIGNED, SEALED
AND DELIVERED

BLUEGRASS
(More or Less)
Volume 1

© 2007 by Robert Blake

<u>Bluegrass More Or Less Vol. 1.</u>

Songs: Big Rock Candy Mountain, Hot Corn, Cold Corn, Rye Whiskey, I'll Be All Smiles Tonight, Pig In A Pen, Buffalo Gals, When Johnny Comes Marching Home, Worried Man Blues, Dixie, Frankie And Johnny, Roll In My Sweet Baby's Arms, Corina-Corina, Shady Grove, Long Journey Home, My Bonnie, Old Time Religion.

(None of my original songs are on this CD)

SIGNED, SEALED
AND DELIVERED

"Dangerous Dan"

"Dr. Bob"

Bonnie

BLUEGRASS
(More or Less)
Volume 2

© 2007 by Robert Blake

Bluegrass More Or Less Vol. 2.

Songs: Columbus Stockade Blues, Sittin' On Top Of The World, Oh, Susannah, New River Train, Wreck Of Old 97, Camptown Races, Shortnin' Bread, Lonesome Road Blues, Polly Wolly Doodle, Take Me Home, Salty Dog Blues, I'm Thinking Tonight Of My Blue Eyes, Froggy Went A-Courtin', Wabash Cannonball, Old Folks At Home, Smoke Hole, Hallelujah I'm Ready.

Smoke Hole. (The only original on this CD)

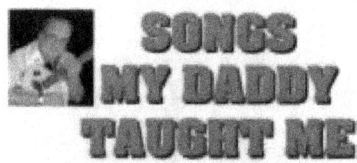

Performed by
BOB BLAKE
aka/"Dr. Bob"/*(The Music Doctor)*
2007

<u>Songs My Daddy Taught Me.</u>

Songs: After The Ball, Alabama Jubilee,
Cuddle Up A Little Closer, Darktown Stutter's Ball,
Hold Your Hand Out Naughty Boy, I Want A Girl,
I Wonder Who's Kissing Her Now, I'm Always
Chasing Rainbows, I'm Forever Blowing Bubbles,
In My Merry Oldsmobile, It's A Long Way
To Tipperary, Let The Rest Of The
World Go By, Loch Lomond, Moonlight Bay,
My Gal Sal, My Wild Irish Rose, Oh Danny Boy,
Put Your Arms Around Me Honey, Shine On Harvest Moon,
Sidewalks Of New York, There's A Long, Long Trail A-
Winding, They Always, Always Pick On Me, Till We Meet
Again, Where The Morning Glories Grow.

MORE SONGS MY DADDY TAUGHT ME

Performed by BOB BLAKE
aka "Dr. Bob" (The Music Doctor)
2007

More Songs My Daddy Taught Me.

Songs: Alexander's Ragtime Band, Bill Bailey,
By The Light Of The Silvery Moon, For Me And My Gal,
In The Shade Of The Old Apple Tree,
Let Me Call You Sweetheart, Margie,
Oh! You Beautiful Doll, Over There, Pretty Baby,
Put On Your Old Gray Bonnet, Row, Row, Row,
School Days, Smoles, Sweet Rosie O'Grady,
That's An Irish Lullaby, The Band Played On,
The Last Long Mile, The Old Gray Mare,
Wait 'Til The Sun Shines Nellie,
When Irish Eyes Are Smiling,
When Johnny Comes Marching Home,
When You Were Sweet 16, Whispering,
You Made Me Love You, You're A Grand Old Flag.

MORE SONGS MY DADDY TAUGHT ME Vol. 2

Performed by BOB BLAKE
aka/"Dr. Bob"(The Music Doctor)

2007

More Songs My Daddy Taught Me Vol. 2.

Songs: America The Beautiful, Around Her Neck She Wore A Yellow Ribbon, Auld Lang Syne, Aura Lee, Barbara Allen, Battle Hymn Of The Republic, Comin' Thro' The Rye, Green Grow The Lilacs, I've Been Working On The Railroad, Ja-da, K-k-k-Katy, Long, Long Ago, My Buddy, O' Columbia The Gem Of The Ocean, Oh Susannah, Old Rosin The Bow, Smile, Smile, Smile, Red White And Blue, The Ash Grove, The Blue-Tail Fly, The Eyes Of Texas Are Upon You, The Roses Are Shining In Picardy, The Yellow Rose Of Texas, There'll Be A HotTime In The Old Town Tonight, There's A Tavern In The Town, Wait For The Wagon, When You Wore A Tulip, Wildwood Flower.

WHERE'S SANTA?

Bob Blake
aka/"Dr. Bob" *(The Music Doctor)*

Where's Santa?

Songs: Where's Santa?, Santa's Comin' Down The Chimney, Mrs. Santa Claus, Christmas Time, Let's All Decorate The Christmas Tree, Rudolph, Christmas n South Florida, My Christmas Tree, Christmas Eve, I'll Be Waiting For Santa Claus.

YOU TURNED ME ON

'DR. BOB' & BONNIE

® © 2008

You Turned Me On.

(This is a Co-Written CD)

Songs: You Turned Me On, I Sing The Songs,
Glory Bound, Hawaii (by the sea of love),
Across The Fields, If Dreams Came True, Love Can,
Baby If The Shoe Fits Wear It, Gentle Country Winds,
Lonely Vacation, Say You'll Be My Friend,
My Beautiful Day.

BOB BLAKE
aka/"Dr. Bob" (The Music Doctor)

<u>**Let's Have Some Fun.**</u>
**Songs: Let's Have Some Fun,
What A Day For Day Dreamin',
Dream A Little Dream Of Tomorrow,
Gimme That Old Boogie Beat, Pickin' And Slidin',
The Burgundy Blues, Good Old Bad Old Country Song, The Frame Of Mind I'm In, I Can't Do A Thing About The Sun, Surfer's Curl, Startin' Over.**

WHAT IF?

BOB BLAKE
aka/"Dr. Bob" *(The Music Doctor)*

What If.

**Songs: What If, Runway, Back To Jamaica,
Ain't Love Grand?, Highland Lassie,
Rocky Road, Rockin' E Blues, Troubled Mind,
Fanciful, Take Me Where I Wanna Be.**

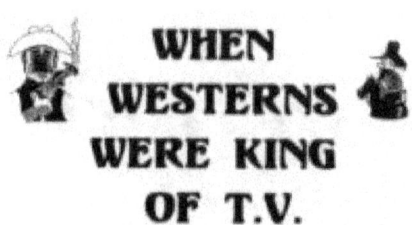

WHEN WESTERNS WERE KING OF T.V.

Bob Blake
aka/"Dr. Bob"
(The Music Doctor)

When Westerns Were King Of T.V.

Songs: When Westerns Were King Of T.V.,
Rollercoaster Junkies,
I Ain't Gonna Work No More,
Hawaii (The Island Of Love).
Mean, Mean Jacquelyne,
Make The Best Of A Bad Situation,
Sailing The Florida Keys,
The Truth,
Daydreamer's Waltz,
Shufflin' Along.

WHERE ARE THE GIRLS?

BOB BLAKE
aka/'Dr Bob'
(The Music Doctor)

℗ © 2008

<u>Where Are The Girls?.</u>

Songs: Where Are The Girls?, Travelin',
You For Me, Through Rolling Hills,
See That Girl, Rockin' Revival,
Sing Me A Dif'rent Kind Of Love Song,
Shufflin' Home, Emeril's Song,
Under The Banyan Tree.

Three Bloomin' Scots.

Songs: Three Bloomin' Scots

(This is the only song of mine on this CD)

Loch Lomond, Aura Lee, Danny Boy,

Hold Your Hand Out Naughty Boy,

My Bonnie, Comin' Thro' The Rye,

Greensleeves, Roamin' In The Gloamin',

Auld Lang Syne.

MASSACHUSETTS

BOB BLAKE
aka/"Dr. Bob" *(The Music Doctor)*

<u>Massachusetts.</u>
Songs: Massachusetts, Any Place Is Home To Me,
Sliding, The Burgundy Blues, Roughshod,
Rainbow Regatta, Troubled Mind,
Wonders, Shufflin' Along, Fort Lauderdale.

BACK WHEN I KNEW ALL THE ANSWERS

BOB BLAKE

aka/"Dr. Bob" (The Music Doctor)

<u>Back When I Knew All The Answers.</u>

Songs: Back When I Knew All The Answers,
Bahama Mama (From Nassau),
I'm Gonna Ask Her In Alaska, Plus, Plus, Also And,
When Your Out-Go Exceeds Your Income,
Time, How Do You Look In Your Birthday Suit?
Down In The Florida Keys,
You Cannot See The Wind, Danny My Boy.

RAPID FINGERS

BOB BLAKE
aka/"Dr. Bob" (The Music Doctor)

Rapid Fingers.

Songs: Rapid Fingers, Smokin' Guitars,
Maelstrom, Running Free,
Roughshod, Daydream,
Dead Reckoning, Epiphany,
Enumeration, Rhythm Of The Waves,
Slightly Diminished.

LET'S UNWIND TONIGHT
"DR. BOB"
&
BONNIE

Let's Unwind Tonight.
(This Is A Co-Written CD)
Songs: Let's Unwind Tonight,
I Wish She Could Read My Mind,
Gotta Get Away From Those Kids,
My Love That Used To Be,
No Baseball Tonight, Mirror,
I Dream Of The Day, Another Blue Song,
Just A Simple Ear-Pleasing Song,
I'm Gonna Go A-Travelin'

Fort Lauderdale.

Songs: Fort Lauderdale, Rollercoaster Junkies,
Sailing The Florida Keys, Back To Jamaica,
Manatee Harbour, The Florida Keys,
Bahama Mama (From Nassau),
Down In The Florida Keys,
Twistin' In The Wind, Yeah, Man!!!.

THERE'S TOO MUCH MONTH AT THE END OF MY MONEY

BOB BLAKE

aka "Dr. Bob" (The Music Doctor)

There's Too Much Month At The End Of My Money.

Songs: There's Too Much Month At The End Of My Money, Baby-Baby-Baby (Slow Version), She Likes To Lallygag, Memories, Please Let Me Go Back To Dreamland, Bing-Bang-Boom, Uncharted Waters, Stepping Stones, It's time, Baby-Baby-Baby (Fast Version).

THE COLORS OF CHRISTMAS

BOB BLAKE

aka/"Dr. Bob" (The Music Doctor)

The Colors Of Christmas.

Songs: The Colors Of Christmas, Santa Is Coming,
Making Angels In The Snow,
The Merry Christmas Blues,
Santa's Coming Pretty Soon,
Joy-Joy It's Christmas Time,
Have Yourself A Merry Christmas,
Jolly Old Elf Named Olaf,
Christmas Is My Favorite Time Of Year,
Christmas Gift Returns.

THE GUNN SQUAD

Robert Blake
aka/"Dr. Bob"
(The Music Doctor)

℗© 2010 by Robert Blake

The Gunn Squad.

Songs: The Gunn Squad, A Cowboy's Life, The Legend Of Falling Rock, Alligator Alli's, I Want you-I Need You-I Love You, Hold Me, Fractured Generation, Emanuelle, Don't Mention My Name, Let's Not Let It End With Broken Hearts.

Robert Blake
aka/"Dr. Bob"
(The Music Doctor)

Dancing On Clouds.

Songs: Dancing On Clouds, I'm Sorry, Jazz Club Ballad, Happy Go Lucky Song, Technology Has Passed Me By, Help, Lo-o-o-o-o-ow Down Blues, Free As A Bird, That Golden Chariot Ride.

Robert Blake aka 'Dr. Bob'
(The Music Doctor)
℗© 2012 by Robert Blake

<u>Upper U.S.</u>

Songs: Upper U.S., It's A Wonderful Life, I Wonder Why, Blow Ye Winds, Sing Me A Song Of Tomorrow, Donna Why, Those Truck Drivin' CB Squallin' Galls, You For Me, While I'm Kneeling Down To Pray, You Don't Have To Be A Star To Be In Our Show.

MEMORIES OF A DRIFTING MIND

by Robert Blake
aka 'Dr. Bob'
(The Music Doctor)

Memories Of A Drifting Mind.

Songs: Memories Of A Drifting Mind, Minor Romp, Like I'm In A Dream, Windward Coast, The Mean Old Florida Blues, The Net, One Track Mind, Slumber, Tornado Toni, Mother Nature-Father Time.

<u>Nuances Of Circumstance.</u>

Songs: Nuances Of Circumstance, Fantasy, We Be Jammin', By My Side, I've Got A Hunger, Speak To Me, Won't You Be My Valentine, It's Never Enough, Come On Baby Do That Number, Today's Your Day.

OPPORTUNITIES

BOB BLAKE

aka/"Dr. Bob" (The Music Doctor)

Opportunities.

Songs: Opportunities, Where Are You Goin',
Park-Shuttle And Fly, I Get Around, Stories,
Yokahama Mama, Congratulations,
If It Weren't For Bad Luck – I'd Have No Luck At All,
Where I'm Goin', Minor Adventure.

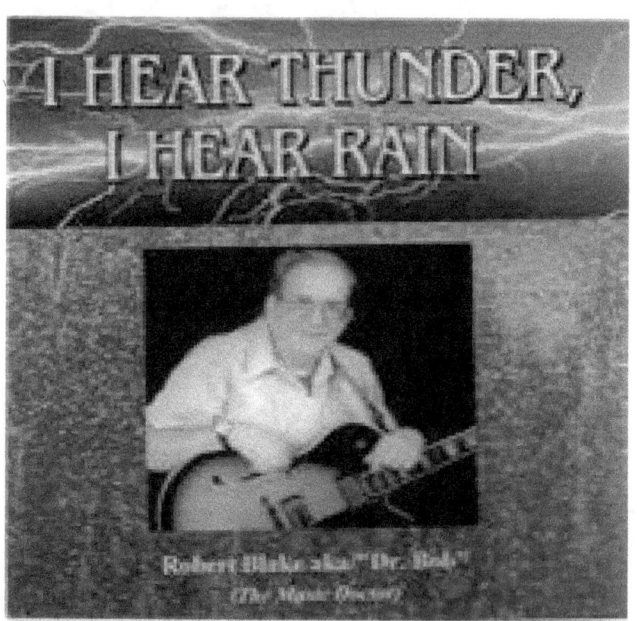

I HEAR THUNDER, I HEAR RAIN

Robert Blake aka "Dr. Bob"
(The Music Doctor)

℗ © 2010 by Robert Blake

I Hear Thunder, I Hear Rain.
Songs: I Hear Thunder-I Hear Rain, Ode To Nature, Disaster In The Gulf Of Mexico, Same Old You, In Good Company, See You Later Baby, Need A Hand, It's Too Late Baby, My Lovable, Huggable, Kissable, Missable You, Sing A Song.

THE CUL DU SAC PARTY

Robert Blake
aka/"Dr. Bob" *(The Music Doctor)*

The Cul Du Sac Party.
Songs: The Cul Du Sac Party,
There's A Full Moon Over Margate,
Have You Ever Wondered?,
Holly-Holly, Winter Storm,
If You'd Only Come To Me,
Sailboat Ride, Too Slow
Donna, It's Too Late,
Happiness.

BLAKE
THE ODD COLOR
ANIMAL FAIR

The Odd Color Animal Fair.

The Odd Color Animal Fair, I'm Jake, The Snake,
Charlie, Queen Of The House, I Am Me,
Exceptional Individuals, Hit Air Baloon,
The Game Of Life, Let's Go To The Carnival,
Polly The Pollywog.

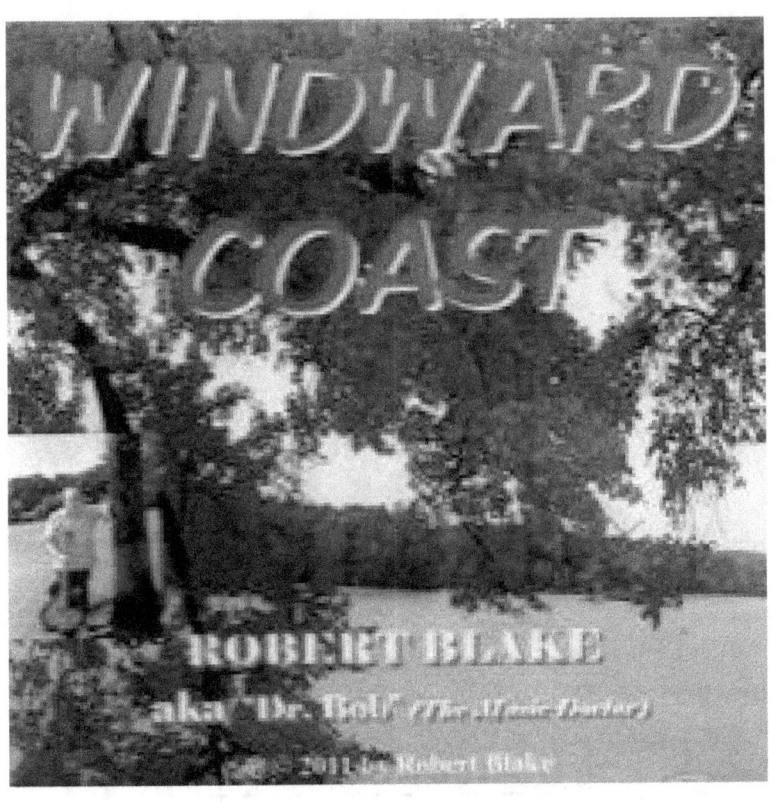

<u>Windward Coast.</u>

Songs: Island Music, Limbo Tonight,
Windward Coast,
Sailboat Ride, Back To Jamaica, Jamaican
Girl, Manatee Harbour,
The Lady From Trinidad, Free As A Bird,
The Girl With The Dreamy Eyes.

The Odd Color Animal Fair II.

Songs: The Odd Color Animal Fair II, Rollercoaster Junkies, Lets Go On A Safari, Can You Imagine Christmas In Australia?, Manatee Harbour, Sing A Little Song, Smaller Than An M&M, Tom Cat, Tools Of The trade, Sing A Song.

BLAKE
My Road To Success Is Under Construction

Robert Blake
aka/'Dr. Bob'
(The Music Doctor)
℗© 2011 by Robert Blake

ROBERT

My Road To Success Is Under Construction.

Songs: My Road To Success Is Under Construction, Cleo's Song, Mutual Love, I'm Out Of Monet-I'm Baroque, You'll Never Know, I'm Just A Hack From Hackensack, Shank's Mare, Lisa, Okydoky, The Faux Song.

TAKE ME TO THE ISLANDS

ROBERT BLAKE
aka/"Dr. Bob" *(The Music Doctor)*

Take Me To The Islands.
(This is a Co-written CD)

Songs: Take Me To The Islands, In And Out Of Love,
Natural Lullaby, Top Of The Hill,
Doin' The Reggae Thing, It's Beach Time.

BLAKE
LET THERE BE MUSIC, LET THERE BE SONG
ROBERT

Robert Blake aka 'Dr. Bob'
The Music Doctor
© 2011 by Robert Blake

Let There Be Music, Let There Be Song.

Songs: Let There Be Music-Let There Be Song,
Baltimore Sue, The Diminished Song, The Million
Dollar Band, Three Little Words, Conundrum 3, I
Dream Of You, A Little Goes A Long-Long Way,
Haunting Melody, Achin'-Breakin' Heart.

ROBERT BLAKE

CAT-AS-TRO-PHE

Robert Blake
aka "Dr. Bob"
The Music Doctor
℗© 2011 by Robert Blake

Cat-As-Tro-Phe.

Songs: Cat-As-Tro-Phe, Amanda-The Panda,
Jag-I-Am, Paula-The Koala Bear, Limbo Tonight,
Lean-Mean Kitty Machine, Bandit, Let'sGo To The Circus,
Olivia, The Gymnasium Song.

ROBERT BLAKE

CHRISTMAS SONGS

Robert Blake aka/'Dr. Bob
(The Music Doctor)

Christmas Songs. (Single)
Song: Christmas Songs.

Robert Blake
aka 'Dr. Bob'
(The Music Doctor)
℗© 2012 by Robert Blake

Today,Tomorrow And Forever.

Songs: Today-Tomorrow And Forever, Indpendent Girl, Property Sculptor, J-o-a-n-n-e, Juli Sunshine, Carmalita-Rosalita-Margarita Del Monico, Our Love Is True Love, And That Is Why, Camille, Out On The Veranda With Miranda.

The Swamp Frog Blues.

Songs: The Swamp Frog Blues, Just Like The Fabled Phoenix, In Heaven There Is A Jamboree, The Picker's Song, Hands, We'll Have A Real Good Time, We Don't Have A Fiddle (But We Sure Fiddle Around), Hither-Thither And Yon, Robin's Egg Blue, Our Love.

ROBERT BLAKE JUNK

Robert Blake
aka 'Dr. Bob'
'The Music Doctor'
®© 2012 by Robert Blake

Junk.

Songs: Junk, Now We Just Moan And Groan,
The Alcan Highway, Self-Righteous Indignation,
Hue And Cry, The Marty Stuart Show,
The Swamp Frog Boogie Beat, Mister Primadonna,
Signologists, We Belong Together.

ROBERT BLAKE
TWO OUT OF THREE AIN'T BAD

Robert Blake
aka 'Dr. Bob'
The Music Doctor
℗© 2012 by Robert Blake

Two Out Of Three Ain't Bad.

Songs: Two Out Of Three Ain't Bad,
I Want To Love You Till The Cows Come Home,
Everything About Her Was The Same,
I Won't Pin You Down To Say "I Love You",
I Love That Girl From Haiti, English Country Star,
Sea Cruiser, There's Never Been A Mother Like You,
Bolo Boogie Beat, Waitin' For The Bills To Come In.

ROBERT BLAKE
SLICK NIK

 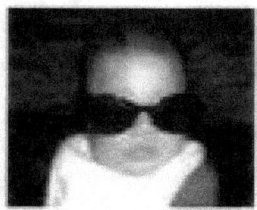

Robert Blake
aka 'Dr. Bob'
(The Music Doctor)

Nikolas Robert Blake
aka 'Slick Nik

Slick Nik.

Songs: Slick Nik, Knock On Grampy's Door,
Nicky In A Bucket, Let's Sing A Song,
The Terror Of 67th Avenue, Rockin' Little Kitty,
Nikolas' Favorite Toy, Niky-Bob,
Milo The Magnificent, 1-800-NIKOLAS,
Sleep-Little Nikolas Sleep.

America,

(The Land Where Freedom Always Rings).

Songs: America,

(The Land Where Freedom Always Rings),

Not Quite Over The Hill Gang,

The Rumerator Song,

I'm Headin' For Miami, Queenie,

Eduardo, Playing With Fire,

The Tigris-The Euphrates-The

Jordan And The Nile,

May The Good Lord Bless You Always,

Lay Me Doon And Dee.

I CAN'T FORGET THE THINGS WE USED TO DO

Robert Blake
aka/"Dr. Bob"
(The Music Doctor)

℗© 2013 by Robert Blake

I Can't Forget The Things We Used To Do.

Songs: I Can't Forget The Things We Used To Do,
The Margate Jump, Up The Golden Staircase,
Jane-Jane-Jane, Rock Me, Picker Man,
Felice And Boudleaux Bryant, Life's Journey,
Pepper Cat, My Counting Song.

ROBERT BLAKE
THE OLD TREE

Robert Blake aka 'Dr. Bob'
The Music Doctor.

℗© 2013 by Robert Blake

The Old Tree.

Songs: The Old Tree, Blues Stay Away From Me,
Wouldn't You Like To Go To See Hawaii?,
I'm Dreamin', Pick Up Your Uke, Phan-Tastic Girl,
They're Just A-Foolin' Around, My Hands,
A Pirate's Life, It's A Long Hard Road To Beulah Land.

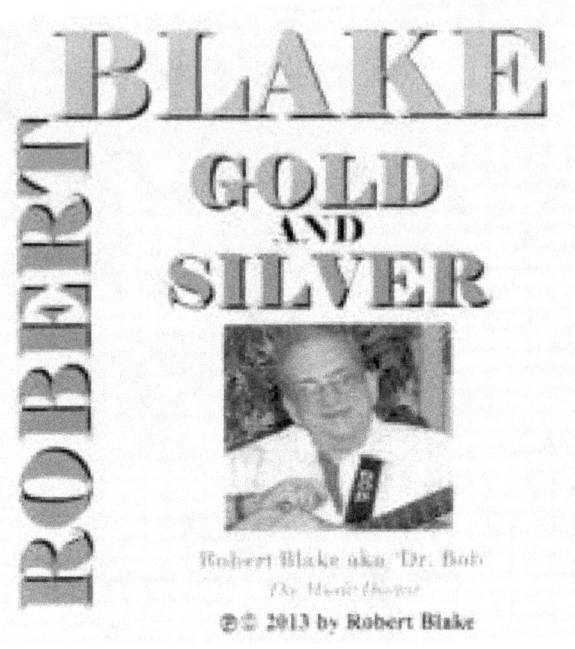

Robert Blake aka "Dr. Bob"
The Music Doctor
℗© 2013 by Robert Blake

Gold And Silver.

Songs: Gold And Silver, Down In The Florida Keys,
Swing Along, The Girl That's In My Dreams,
She's Clowning Around,
Waiting For The Other Shoe To Drop,
Directions, Companion To The Blues,
Time Will Tell, You Can't.

Mister Cab Driver (Single)
Song: Mister Cab Driver.

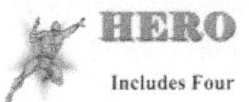

Includes Four

Fast Action Hero.

Songs: Fast Action Hero, Gold Wheels And
Purple Lug Nuts, Cold Today-Hot Tamale,
I Can't See Me Lovin' Nobody But You,
My Rowing Queen, Smoke On The Desert-Fire In
The Sky, American Indian, Water-Wind-Fire And Rock,
Harding Street Waltz, I Love The Islands,
Disaster In the Gulf Of Mexico,
Technology Has Passed Me By,
Halloween Night, Ghosts And Goblins,
Haunting Melody, Slightly Diminished,
Gold Wheels And Purple Lug Nuts (Instrumental).

MAKE THOSE JINGLE BELLS ROCK

Robert Blake aka/"Dr. Bob"
(The Music Doctor)
℗© 2013 by Robert Blake

<u>Make Those Jingle Bells Rock.</u>
Songs: Make Those Jingle Bells Rock,
Santa Claus Rock, I'm Dreaming Of A
Christmas That Is White,
Another Christmas Season,
Our Snowman Wasn't Frosty,
Rockin' Christmas Party,
Bubba-The Buck-Tooth Reindeer,
S*N*O*W, Winter Time,
C*H*R*I*S*T*M*A*S.

WHEELS
2014

Robert Blake aka/"Dr. Bob"
The Music Doctor

℗© 2014 by Robert Blake

Wheels 2014.

Songs: Wheels 2014, In The Good Old Ancient World, Crammin' Duet, Bella-Bella-Bella, She's A Mean One, I Believe In Zinfandel, Cool Side Of The Pillow, Zumba With Zulma, Hands Were Made For Holding, She's A Keeper, Underwear Jack.

"Dr, Bob's" Triple Pack.

Contains 1 a DVD Featuring Guitar Instruction,
1 CD with the song lyrics with the chords
& 1 CD with jpg pictures of the pages of my Guitar
Instruction book "By The Book".

"DR. BOB'S"
BEGINNER GUITAR
Open "G" Tuning

"Dr. Bob's" Beginner Guitar
Using The Open G Tuning.

Contains how to tune your guitar,
chording and much more.

"Dr. Bob's" Beginner Guitar Vol. 1.

Contains the audio for your first 8 weeks of guitar
instruction.

DR. BOB'S
BEGINNER GUITAR
Volume Two

Bob Blake
aka "Dr. Bob"
(The Music Doctor)

Audio taken from "Dr. Bob's" Triple Pack DVD
& CD package.
Copyright 2004 by Robert Blake

"Dr. Bob's" Beginner Guitar Vol. Two.

Contains a review of Vol. 1 and the instruction for your second set of 8 week of learning the guitar.

---

25 Steps To Boost Your Songwriting, Performing and Recording Career.

This CD Contains helpful information for Performers, Singer/Songwriters & even Poets.

<u>Christmas Guitar,</u>
Songs: Away In A Manger,
Bring A Torch Jeanette Isabella,
Deck The Halls, God Rest Ye Merry
Gentlemen, Good Christian Men Rejoice, Good King
Wenceslas, Hark The Herald Angels Sing,
Here We Come A-Wassailing,
It Came Upon The Midnight Clear,
Jingle Bells, Joy To The World,
O' Christmas Tree, O' Come All Ye Faithful,
O' Holy Night, O' Little Town Of Bethlehem,
Silent Night, The First Noel,
The Holly And The Ivy,
Up On The House Top, We Three Kings,
We Wish You A Merry Christmas, What Child Is This.

<u>Traditional Christmas Songs.</u>
Songs: O' Little Town Of Bethlehem,
The First Noel, We Three Kings, ,
Hark The Herald Angels Sing,
It Came Upon The Midnight Clear,
Away In A Manger, Joy To The World,
O' Come All Ye Faithful,
Up On The House Top, Deck The Halls,
O' Holy Night, Jingle Bells, Silent Night,

TRADITIONAL SACRED SONGS
Volume One

Performed by
BOB BLAKE
aka/"Dr. Bob"*(The Music Doctor)*

Traditional Sacred Songs Volume One.

Songs: Abide With Me. Amazing Grace,
Blest Be The Tie That Binds, Fairest Lord Jesus,
Holy-Holy-Holy, In The Garden, Battle Hymn Of
The Republic, Faith Of Our Fathers,
Kub-bah-ya, Onward Christian Soldiers,
Joyful-Joyful We Adore Thee,
Rock Of Ages, Softly And Tenderly,
This I My Fathers World, What If It Were Today.

TRADITIONAL SACRED SONGS

Volume Two

Performed by
BOB BLAKE
aka/"Dr. Bob"(The Music Doctor)

<u>Traditional Sacred Songs Volume Two.</u>
Songs: Bringing In The Sheaves, Jesus Loves Me, Let Us Break Bread Together, Old Time Religion, The Old Rugged Cross, The Church In The Wildwood, What A Friend We Have In Jesus, Will The Circle Be Unbroken, Stand Up-Stand Up For Jesus, Beautiful Isle Of Somewhere, Christ The Lord Is Risen Today, Come Ye Thankful People Come, Praise God From Whom All Blessings Flow, This Joyful Easter Tide, Swing Low Sweet Chariot.

Performed by
PAT UBER & BOB BLAKE
aka/"Dr. Bob"*(The Music Doctor)*

Ⓟ © 2009 by Pat Uber & Robert Blake

Favorite Songs.

Songs: Do Lord, In The Garden, Jesus Loves Me, Just A Closer Walk With Thee, Kum-Bah-Ya, Old Time Religion, Softly And Tenderly, What A Friend We Have In Jesus, The Old Rugged Cross, Amazing Grace.

Introducing:

STEPPING STONES

BOB BLAKE
aka/"Dr. Bob"(The Music Doctor)
BOB CHALICH &DAN BARROW

Introducing: Stepping Stones:

Bob Chalich, Bob Blake & Dan Barrow.

Songs: Worried Man Blues, This Little Light Of Mine, Shenandoah, Good News, Kum-bah-ya, When The Saints Go Marching In, Amazing Grace, This Nine Pound Hammer, Bill Bailey, Swing Low Sweet Chariot.

Stepping Stones.

Uncharted Waters.

Songs: Stepping Stones, Uncharted Waters, Katie Did, There's Too Much Month At The End Of My Money, She Likes To Lallygag, Bing-Bang-Boom-Baby-Baby, Please Let Me Go Back To Dreamland, Memories, It's Time.

STEPPING STONES
Christmas Favorites Vol. 1

Stepping Stones.

Christmas Favorites Vo. 1.

Songs: Away In A Manger, Bring A Torch Jeanette Isabella, Deck The Halls, Hark! The Herald Angels Sing, It Came Upon The Midnight Clear, Jingle Bells, O' Little Town Of Bethlehem, We Three Kings, Silent Night, We Wish You A Merry Christmas.

Written and Performed by
Bob Blake aka/"Dr. Bob" (The Music Doctor)
& Nisa McCall

℗© 2010 by Robert Blake & Nisa McCall

The Shout Out No More Bullying Song.
(This is a Single)
Written and recorded by
Robert Blake
aka/"Dr. Bob" (The Music Doctor) and
Nisa McCall.

Robert Blake aka/'Dr. Bob'
The Music Doctor

HEAVENS
TO BETSY!!!

℗© 2015 by Robert Blake

Heaven's To Betsy.

Songs: Heavens To Betsy, Diana's Bananas,
Yankee From New England,
Ditto Me Baby, I Love Pizza, Train Ride,
Me Myself And I, Winters Get Cold,
Writing A Song Can Be Easy,
Life Is A Journey, My Life.

Robert Blake aka 'Dr. Bob'
(The Music Doctor)

DAYS

and

NIGHTS

℗© 2015 by Robert Blake

Days And Nights.
Songs: Days And Nights,
Old Mister Shade, Snowflakes,
Gloria Jean, Annie's Phantastic,
Recipe or A Party, Two Little Goats,
Lourdes, Movin' To The Music,
She's A Jewish Cowgirl From Brooklyn.

www.ingramcontent.com/pod-product-compliance
Lightning Source LLC
Chambersburg PA
CBHW070313290526
45791CB00003B/1112